Dedication

When I was a kid, I was accused of being "ungrateful" by an amazing family friend. The accusation hurt deeply because I sure *felt* grateful. On pondering the conversation with her, I realized that she was right. Even though I felt grateful, I didn't verbalize it, so she had no idea! I made a decision from that moment forward to start to verbalize my gratitude.

This family friend was deeply engaged in our church life by directing the choir, helping with the kids' program and being an all-around cool person. She gave my brother his first car. She took teens to the coolest outdoor Spirit-fest concert ever in Wilmore, Kentucky and also gave me a personal scholarship of $1000 when I went to college! She was also a running buddy for my mom and me and helped us train for our first 10K.

Wow! What a giving individual! Her name was Jama Martin and she blessed my life and the life of my family over and over. Thank you - I am deeply grateful.

Jama Martin, this book is dedicated to you.

Introduction

A Grateful Life: 30 Days of Conscious Gratitude is a tool to be used as you move forward on your spiritual journey. It is to serve as a reminder that all good gifts are from God and as we focus on this good, it expands.

Take time each day to pause and reflect on the day's lesson. Breathe deeply. Light a candle. Say a prayer. Create a sacred ritual around your time of gratitude. Remember that God's will for you is good!

My prayer for you this season is that you will know God's abundance and begin to share it with all you meet.

You are loved.

You are supported.

You are blessed.

In humble gratitude,

Rev. Cynthia Alice Anderson

A Grateful Life: 30 Days of Conscious Gratitude

by Rev. Cynthia Alice Anderson

with photographs by Casandra Akins

DAY 1 - Affirmation: Today, I claim my abundance! I am grateful.

Thank you God, for all that I have been given. My home, my family, my life and my work bless me.

I take time right now to envision all the blessings in my life. I name them and give thanks. Thank you, God. Thank you, God. Thank you, God.

I am loved. I am supported. I am blessed. I am grateful.

DAY 2 - Affirmation: Thank you, God! Thank you, God! Thank you, God! I am grateful.

My life and my work include so much goodness from God. Today, I will take time to list just 10 of the wonderful things God has given me. I know the scriptures proclaim:

> *"Every generous act of giving, with every perfect gift, is from above, coming down from the Father of lights, with whom there is no variation of shadow due to change." James 1:17, (NRSV)*

I know this means that all the good in my life is from God and I am grateful.

I am loved. I am supported. I am blessed. I am grateful.

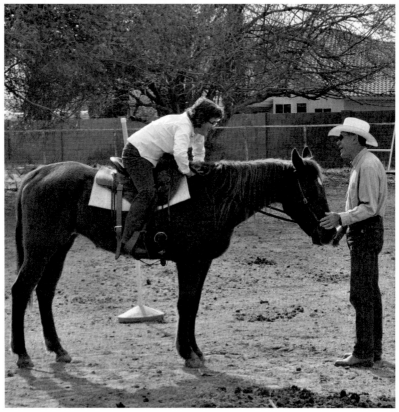

DAY 3 - Affirmation: Thank you, God, for the people who bless my life! I am grateful.

Today I am mindful of all the individuals who have blessed me on my spiritual journey. My teachers have been many and some of them came to me when I least expected but definitely needed it. Thank you, God, for the people who bless my life.

Today I will reach out and contact three people who bless me. I will extend my love and gratitude for their support of my life energy.

I am loved. I am supported. I am blessed. I am grateful.

DAY 4 - Affirmation: Thank you, God, for all those who help me! I am grateful.

Today as I go to the store or pick up my cleaning, or just have a coffee, I will make a special effort to thank those in service to me. I realize that an extra kindness, a smile, or a really good tip will brighten someone's day. I have so much gratitude, I can't wait to share it! Thank you, God for those who help and support me in my daily life.

I am loved. I am supported. I am blessed. I am grateful.

DAY 5 - Affirmation: God is my Source of all abundance. I am grateful.

Thank you, God, for all my financial resources. I am grateful for my work and for proper compensation for what I do. I use my finances for good and give 10% to the place of my spiritual nourishment. I know I work for God and all money comes to me through different avenues. God is my Source of all abundance.

I am loved. I am supported. I am blessed. I am grateful.

DAY 6 - Affirmation: My family blesses me every day. I am grateful.

Every day, I am reminded of God's goodness to me when I look in the eyes of the ones I love. I see God's love shining back through them to bless me. I see God's light shining in them as they clean their room, work around the house, or cook dinner. I am so grateful for my family and their presence in my life and in the world.

I am loved. I am supported. I am blessed. I am grateful.

DAY 7 - Affirmation: Thank you God, for my home. I am grateful.

My home blesses me daily as I get ready for work, return home to make dinner, and do my spiritual work. My home blesses and enfolds me and keeps me safe. It nurtures me when I am there, misses me when I depart, and welcomes me home when I return. I must remember that all parts of my home are living - they have a soul.

Today, I will bless my home with sacred words and sacred actions. All I do in my home is sacred. As I do my spiritual work today, I speak affirmations aloud to bless my home. Thank you, God, for my home.

I am loved. I am supported. I am blessed. I am grateful.

DAY 8 - Affirmation: Thank you, God, that I can be of service. I am grateful.

When I have so much, it's natural to want to serve. I give from my abundance. I ask Spirit's guidance today on where and how I need to share my gifts and talents. I know I am being guided. God's will for me is good. God works through me to bless others.

Whether at work or home, whomever I serve, I am ultimately serving God.

I am loved. I am supported. I am blessed. I am grateful.

DAY 9 - Affirmation: Today all my actions are sacred. I am grateful.

I remember that everything I do is sacred because I am sacred. My actions are sacred and conscious as I look for ways to make a difference. I desire to be the person that brightens someone's day with a kind word, a well-thought card, or a hug at just the right time.

Today God guides me and I am sacred.

I am loved. I am supported. I am blessed. I am grateful.

DAY 10 - Affirmation: I speak words of gratitude and blessing. I am grateful.

I take time to speak my words of gratitude today. My family, coworkers, and those I live with bless me daily. It's time to say, "Thank you for blessing me!" Or ,"I love you and am so grateful for you! You bless me every day." A note in someone's lunch or in your spouse's work bag or calendar can be a totally unexpected blessing. And you will be amazed at how good you feel doing it! Share the love - be grateful and speak it!

I am loved. I am supported. I am blessed. I am grateful.

DAY 11 - Affirmation: Thank you, God, for my country. I am grateful.

I am reminded today that both men and women give their lives in service to this county. I am grateful to live in a country that values freedom and justice. My prayer is that our nation and its leaders seek God first in their decision-making.

I honor our nation and our nation's leaders. I am grateful for those who serve our country.

I am loved. I am supported. I am blessed. I am grateful.

DAY 12 - Affirmation: Thank you, God, for the peacemakers. I am grateful.

There are those in our country and around the world who serve us through thoughts, meditations, and peaceful actions. People and leaders of every faith lift up our world, seeing peace for all. I am grateful for the peacemakers.

Today I envision peace in every aspect of my life, community and the world. I believe peace is possible.

I am loved. I am supported. I am blessed. I am grateful.

DAY 13 - Affirmation: Thank you, God, for faith! I am grateful.

One of my God- given gifts is the gift of faith. I have all that I need. The scriptures tell us in Hebrews 11:1,

> *"Now faith is the assurance of things hoped for, the conviction of things not seen." (NRSV)*

My spiritual work is to exercise my faith by seeing what is possible in any given situation. As I exercise my faith, I am grateful. I use my faith to rely more on God and move forward on my spiritual journey.

I am loved. I am supported. I am blessed. I am grateful.

DAY 14 - Affirmation: Thank you, God, for the gift of love. I am grateful.

I am blessed each day by the ability to love and be loved. Love is a gift from God. My prayer today is to be love in every situation.

As I drive, work, play, cook or just be, I am love. Love is my true nature and I am grateful.

I am loved. I am supported. I am blessed. I am grateful.

DAY 15 - Affirmation: Thank you, God, for where I live! I am grateful.

My great state has beautiful weather and gorgeous trees. The birds sing each morning and awaken me with gentle melodies and sweet chirps. The squirrels entertain me with their finesse and antics.

I enjoy where I live and the nature that surrounds me. I am grateful for all these gifts from God.

Today I will thank the birds and the squirrels and the trees for blessing me. I will also thank God for the blessings they are. I am grateful.

I am loved. I am supported. I am blessed. I am grateful.

DAY 16 - Affirmation: Thank you, God, for my community. I am grateful.

The community in which I live, work and worship, supports me. I chose this community consciously and I am grateful for the Divine guidance that brought me here.

Today I will ask Spirit's guidance on how I can show my gratitude for these important areas of my life: where I live, work and worship. My intention is to live a grateful life.

I am loved. I am supported. I am blessed. I am grateful.

DAY 17 - Affirmation: I work for God! I am grateful.

Whether I earn a paycheck, am on retirement or even disability, I work for God. Everything I do is for God and about God. All the work I do is holy.

My conversations, phone calls, emails and meetings are filled with God-energy. I continuously acknowledge God as the Source of all good. I work for God.

I am loved. I am supported. I am blessed. I am grateful.

DAY 18 - Affirmation: The school of life has taught me much. I am grateful.

Each situation in life is an opportunity to grow and expand. My intention is to live consciously and love myself enough to learn from the past. As I learn from the past, I bring new learning and awareness into the present.

Today I will see a perceived problem as a soul opportunity. I am becoming conscious, breathing into the moment, and being present to the present.

Life is a gift from God. I am learning and growing in this earth school. Thank you, God, for guiding me.

I am loved. I am supported. I am blessed. I am grateful.

DAY 19 - Affirmation: I am safe and protected. I am grateful.

Thank you, God for those who protect and serve. The police officers, firefighters, doctors and nurses of my community support me. I know they work to keep me safe and protected.

I am being guided daily by God in all my affairs. I will take steps to protect myself when needed and I will call on support for this important work.

I am loved. I am supported. I am blessed. I am grateful.

DAY 20 - Affirmation: Thank you God, for those who serve my community with great love! I am grateful.

I am mindful of the teachers, social workers, therapists and counselors who serve my family and the greater community. I am confident they are holding the high watch for our children, families and the world.

I will reach out to thank those in service to acknowledge their service as a gift from God. I realize the difference they make daily and I am grateful.

I am loved. I am supported. I am blessed. I am grateful.

DAY 21 - Affirmation: My friends bless me with laughter, support and love. I am grateful.

The James Taylor song, "You've God A Friend" is an old favorite and brings to mind a true friend. If you are in need, you will only call a true friend.

True friends are those who share life's highest highs and lowest lows. They love and support you as you navigate this life, this earth school. A true friend is a gift from God.

Make a mental inventory of who you consider to be a true friend. Then, reach out by phone and ask if they would be willing to be an official member of your support team. When you receive your answers, make a list and post it on your refrigerator so you can look at it all the time. Remember how supported you are! And don't forget to thank your support team - show your gratitude!

I am loved. I am supported. I am blessed. I am grateful.

Day 22 - My animals bless me. I am grateful.

*"As I watch my cat look for and find a sun patch to lie down in, I smile.
This cat teaches me self-love like no human ever could. He is always
making sure he's comfortable and happy with plenty to eat and lots of sleep.
And when he's ready for love, he asks for it and gets it!"*

I learn every day from the animals in my life. I am grateful for their spirits and personalities that bless me daily. I thank God for the animals in my life.

I am loved. I am supported. I am blessed. I am grateful.

DAY 23 - Affirmation: Mother Earth supports me with everything I need. I am grateful.

A beautiful morning ritual is to wake up gently, asking Mother Earth how she is holding you today, then listen for the answer. You may be surprised at first, but you will grow accustomed to it. Our earth has an energy and a consciousness.

She wants to speak to you.

Take a few moments today to notice how much the earth gives you - everything - for free. You have all the sun you need, all the oxygen to breathe. Step outside and feel and listen. Thank her for her goodness to you.

Get quiet and listen to the wind and the trees speak back.

I am loved. I am supported. I am blessed. I am grateful.

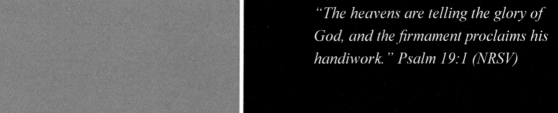

*"The heavens are telling the glory of
God, and the firmament proclaims his
handiwork." Psalm 19:1 (NRSV)*

**Day 24 - The sun, moon and stars bless
me daily. I am grateful.**

"It was a tradition in my family growing
up that all of the children were taught to
look at the night sky and know, name and
find the constellations. We could not wait
for warmer temperatures which frequently
meant sleeping outside, where we would
often drift off to sleep while scanning the
night sky for shooting stars. I always felt
those stars were a safe place for me, a
home. I have taught my son the same. He
also sees the stars as his ancestors guiding
the way."

During the day I use an affirmation
every time I feel the sun on my face, "I
am made of light. I am designed to be a
master and to live that in the world."

I am loved. I am supported. I am blessed.
I am grateful.

DAY 25 - Affirmation: Thank you God, for my spiritual teachers and mentors. I am grateful.

A popular quote that I particularly love says,

> *"When the student is ready, the teacher appears."*

What a true statement! God is working in every aspect of your life to bless you and move you into wholeness. God can only bless you at the level you are ready.

If you don't think you have a spiritual teacher right now look around - consciously. They may not be a minister or spiritual master by profession. They may be a spouse, coworker, therapist or friend. Their words may be guiding you. Or a conflict may be showing you an area of growth. Be open and grateful for the teaching!

I am grateful for my spiritual teachers.

I am loved. I am supported. I am blessed. I am grateful.

DAY 26 - Affirmation: Thank you God, for my soul. I am grateful.

Your soul is guiding you daily, hourly, momently. Many times you will not be aware of it but an intuitive or "gut" feeling or knowing about something is the language of your soul. Take time today to be quiet and listen to your soul. The more you get to know its voice, the more abundant and guided your life will be.

I take time today to thank my soul for guiding me.

I am loved. I am supported. I am blessed. I am grateful.

DAY 27 - Affirmation: My spiritual community blesses me daily. I am grateful.

Each week I attend church, I feel God's presence and power working in and through my life. I acknowledge it. I thank the people who continue to support me with prayers, music and uplifting messages.

I remember God's will for me is good. As I acknowledge the good in my spiritual community, that goodness will seek to follow me!

I ask God's guidance today on how I can show my love and gratitude for all my spiritual nourishment.

I am loved. I am supported. I am blessed. I am grateful.

DAY 28 - Affirmation: I see everything as sacred. I am grateful.

Every moment is a sacred moment. Everything is sacred. As I sit and relax, I notice the things around me. Everything is filled with the light of God. I envision things the way they are: sacred and full of light.

As I prepare to move into my day, I remember to walk humbly and with great nobility. An ancient Serbian proverb says,

> *"Be humble for you are made of earth. Be noble for you are made of stars."*

Everything is sacred and I am sacred.

I am loved. I am supported. I am blessed. I am grateful.

DAY 29 - Affirmation: Thank you, God, for being God! I am grateful.

I am grateful each day and moment for the power of God in my life. I continue to see miracles happen and opportunities present themselves to help me grow. My soul knows God and listens to God momently.

I see God everywhere and know God is blessing me now! I claim God's goodness in my life and I am grateful.

I am loved. I am supported. I am blessed. I am grateful.

Day 30 - I move forward on my spiritual journey. I am grateful.

Thank you, God, for supporting me every moment of every day! My soul is happy, blessed, joyous and free. I feel God's love uplifting me in this moment and always.

I act in the best interest of my soul by doing my spiritual work. I take time daily to pray, meditate, sing, and forgive. My soul is leading me forward and I am so grateful.

I am loved. I am supported. I am blessed. I am grateful.